# Beating YouTube

0 to 1000 Subscribers In Under 30 Days

By Joshua Baldwin

© 2023 All Rights Reserved

# Contents

# Abstract

Have you ever seen someone making content online for a living and thought to yourself… wait… it's that easy?! Have you ever pictured yourself doing exactly what you saw them doing, but better? When it comes to building sustainable, long-term growth in business, and even life in general, it's important to learn *how to market yourself*. And in this hyper-consumerist society we live in, *one of the most powerful marketing platforms that billions of people use around the world today, is YouTube.* I'm here to show you the *REAL* strategies and methods needed to scale your very own YouTube channel to 1000 subscribers in less than 30 days! In fact, by applying these tactics, I personally hit this milestone by only my sixth video on one of my YouTube channels. I'm not here to drag on with any motivational monologues or sound bites you've heard from countless so-called "marketing gurus." What I'm here to tell you is the cold, hard truth about how to succeed on YouTube. And provide you with a comprehensive step-by-step guide on how to start your own YouTube channel and grow it from 0 to 1000 subscribers. The time to grow is different for everyone, but if you follow the rules and strategies laid out in this book, it is 100% possible for anyone to succeed at this. This book will also teach you how to smoothly scale your channel in the shortest possible time. As a Creator, I have studied YouTube's analytics for many years. In that time, I have amassed a fair amount of knowledge and experience, which I am proud to now share with all of YOU! So, if you're reading this, *congratulations on taking the first step on the right path to financial security!*

Your decision to read this is one of the wisest decisions you will ever make, as *the tips laid out in this book will guarantee you a YouTube channel that will earn you some serious $$$.* If you take the time to closely follow the principles I am about to discuss, you will set yourself up for serious success. A monetized YouTube channel is a beautiful thing because it's like having a separate bank account. One that continues to earn you money, even while you're sleeping. Otherwise known as passive income. Module 1 of this book will be focused on *choosing a niche and confidently believing in it*. Module 2 will demonstrate *a complete procedure for setting up and optimizing your first-ever YouTube channel*, everything from designing your channel art to choosing a stunning profile image. Module 3 will be focused on *how to design your videos to maximize their visibility in the eyes of your audience and by the almighty YouTube algorithm*. And finally, our fourth and final module will cover *the full video upload process, including effective techniques designed to maximize the visibility of your channel and overall BRAND!*

This book aims to provide you with the mindset, skills, and strategies to establish your very own

YouTube channel and scale it from 0 to 1000 subscribers the fastest. Without further ado, let's get into it.

*"Without commitment you'll never start. Without consistency you'll never finish…"*

-Denzel Washington

# Module 1: Choosing Your Niche... AND BELIEVING IN IT!

The first step is choosing your niche. Why? Well, how are you going to make videos if you don't know what to make videos about? If you want to succeed at this, you must inevitably come to terms with something. Your first video idea is likely amateurish at best. If you think you're an expert already... you're wrong. But I applaud you anyway for showing initiative. In saying that, you need to forget everything you thought you knew previously about making money on YouTube. 99.99% of the content you read and watch online consists largely of recycled nonsense that countless scammers have mentioned repeatedly for monetary gain. How many marketing influencers have you heard that taught you anything of *REAL* substance or value? This guide will provide you with a complete set of tools needed to get you set up with a profitable YouTube business.

Remember that rarely is a YouTuber's first-ever video the most successful or viral one of their career. In fact, your first video will often yield some of your lowest views simply because YouTube has not yet had the opportunity to learn what your channel is about or what kind of content you put out there. It could take 10 videos. It could take 100 videos. But if you follow the strategies that I'm about to share with you, you will at least minimize the time to reach your goals. Not only that, but the more you practice them, the better you'll get. Before you know it, creating and posting videos will become almost like a sixth sense and feel natural to you.

So how do you figure out whether your video or channel idea is worth pursuing? What if you don't have a clue where to start? Well, that's why I'm here. To be the random force of nature that solves all your problems. Let's jump into a few different scenarios, each based on two factors: general searchability and confidence level in your channel's direction.

# SCENARIO 1: You have an idea for a channel that ISN'T highly searchable, but you are 100% focused on starting it anyways…

**Solution**: In this scenario, there are two key ideas you will need to grasp if you want to succeed. You must both:

(1) LOVE Your Niche.

And…

(2) BELIEVE in it.

Let's stop here and think about this. *To make money doing YouTube, you simply won't go far unless you believe in yourself.* This scenario will likely be the most challenging for you if you're not already a naturally charming or charismatic online personality. If you can't attract a general audience to your videos, you will be forced to lean more on your cult following to grow your channel. This isn't always ideal for growth because it prevents you from tapping into much wider-reaching sources of traffic, like YouTube recommendations. Unless your niche is already highly searched or trending, you will find it almost impossible to tap into YouTube recommendations or gain any sustainable long-term growth. If your video topics aren't highly searchable, your channel will lack the ability to gain the same number of YouTube recommendations as a channel that targets the most trending content. YouTube specifically aims to promote channels that post videos on popular or trending topics, in order to maximize their ad sharing revenue.

# SCENARIO 2: You have an idea for a channel you AREN'T SURE is highly searchable…

**Solution:** If you're unsure and want to confirm whether your channel idea has promise, a good way to verify this is performing a simple search for any other big YouTubers in your niche. YouTubers with around 500k subscribers are about the range you should be searching for, but preferably at least 1M+. Check out the video titles and see if any of them resemble anything close to the style or theme of your videos. From there, check the views those videos are receiving. Generally, if they're in the hundreds of thousands, there's a good bet you've struck gold with your chosen niche. This will provide you with the social proof needed to confirm your niche is popular amongst the people. There are several excellent tools out there for you to try if you genuinely need help and have no idea what people are interested in. There's Google Trends for analyzing popular Google search data. If you want to home in on what people are searching for on YouTube specifically, TubeBuddy is also a great option for Creators. Even the free version offers tools that help you select the highest trending and search-optimized titles and tags to use for your videos. In fact, using TubeBuddy is something I practice religiously to ensure I always achieve the highest SEO score possible on my videos.

# SCENARIO 3: You have an idea for a highly searchable channel on the internet…

**Solution**: If you're confident that you have your niche nailed down and are ready to start making content right away, feel free to skip this module and move ahead to the next one. Just to be sure, I still suggest you follow all the steps I explained above in *SCENARIO 2.*

# SCENARIO 4: You have no idea what you want to make your channel about…

**Solution:** If you have zero ideas on how to form your first-ever YouTube channel, there is a solution. Later in this book and as a gift to all my readers, I am going to reveal a channel content idea that is guaranteed to get you monetized, so you start earning money right away. You're welcome… Aren't you glad you read this book now? But in all seriousness, this can be a decent opportunity for you… Especially if you're someone as busy as me and don't have the time or energy to continuously come up with new content, day in and day out. Maybe you already have a primary source of income and see this more as a side hustle. If that's the case, I 100%

agree with you. With YouTube, it's often NOT a good idea to put all your eggs in one basket. You should view YouTube as a means to grow a profitable side business, NOT as a primary source of income. That is…until it becomes big enough to become your main source of income. YouTube is not by any stretch a perfectly oiled machine. If you imagined yourself posting videos and magically getting the same kind of traffic each time, you couldn't be more wrong. Furthermore, if you base all your satisfaction on your ability to achieve the same numbers of views on every single video, you will be severely disappointed. Receiving more, or less views, on one video than another, is commonplace on the YouTube platform and something you must get used to, especially if you want to maintain a level head while doing this. YouTube can be quite the emotional ride, and the only way to ensure you don't throw in the towel before you pick up momentum and make some real money is by #1, following the principles and tips I've laid out in this book. And #2, keeping calm and keeping on. Remember… *consistency is key in this game.*

Don't waste too much time choosing a niche, either. You have limited time on this Earth. Make a bold decision about your channel's subject matter, stick with it, and don't look back. Once you've chosen your niche and are happy with it, you are ready to move on to Module 2, where we will discuss how to create your first-ever YouTube channel. And how to optimize it for maximum visibility.

*"Everything you've ever wanted is on the other side of fear…"*

-George Adair

# Module 2: Channel & Video Search Engine Optimization

Hello and welcome to Module 2, where we will explore: Channel and Video Search Engine Optimization. In this section, I will demonstrate exactly how you can create your first-ever YouTube channel. And how to optimally design each component to ensure it gets recognized by a large audience. The more optimized your YouTube channel is, the easier it is for your potential subscribers to find you. This ultimately leads to more channel exposure, and the benefits multiply. We will also discuss precisely how you can optimize your videos for YouTube search. With your channel and videos optimized, you greatly improve your chances of becoming a competitive brand and reaching wider audiences. The goal here is to get you from 0 to 1000 subscribers. And ideally, in less than 30 days. Because who wants to wait longer than that? This is not supposed to feel like the line at the DMV! Making videos is supposed to be fun and relaxing!

Alright, enough chitter-chatter. Let's get down to the nitty-gritty...

There are 3 main components you need to pay attention to when building an extraordinary YouTube channel:

The first component will be focused on your channel art, which most notably includes your banner.

## 1. Channel Cover Art / Banner

"Why should your subscribers follow your videos?" That is essentially the question you'll want to answer with your channel banner. Remember, your banner appears at the very top of your channel. And so, it will take up a significant portion of people's screen space on their phone, computer, TV, or any other device. You need to make it POP!

The first thing to remember regarding your channel banner is sizing. According to YouTube, the ideal banner size is 2560 x 1440 pixels. So how in the heck do we create a banner that #1) looks incredible AND #2) fits these sizing requirements? You have a couple of options for creating and sizing your banner correctly. And each option demands a different kind of budget...

I.  The first option is 100% free. And that's to design your own banner picture on a basic computer program like Microsoft Paint or Word. Then crop it. Save it as a JPG or PNG somewhere on your Desktop. And iteratively edit and shape it to fit the YouTube banner size requirement. Now, I'll be the first to admit that this method is challenging and can take quite a few tries. Often, the image will appear misaligned, the text will end up in the wrong place, and it can become pixelated once it gets stretched after upload.

II.   The next option for creating a banner, which comes with a small cost, is to hire a freelance design artist on a website like Fiverr or Upwork. That way, a seasoned professional can create your banner on your behalf. This is probably the easiest and best option because you barely need to lift a finger. And out the other side, you'll have a stunning banner. One thing to remember, though, if you decide to go this route, make sure your freelancer agrees to hand over the rights to the image. Typically, they will do this by default, but it's not a bad idea to check regardless to protect you from any potential future copyright infringement.

## 2. Channel Icon / Profile Image

There isn't a whole lot of mystery to this one. If you're an individual or a personal brand, a nice friendly picture of your face will be sufficient. Or, if you're a business, you'll probably want to add your logo here. In terms of sizing, you'll want your image to be 800 x 800 pixels.

Now let's stop to identify what these two items we mentioned represent clearly... *YOUR BRAND!!!* Your channel art and profile photo are two of *THE most crucial components to the success of your channel.* Think about how you will present yourself to your audience and other companies that could potentially partner with you in doing brand deals. The world is saturated and full of people trying to outshine each other, so the only way to survive in this hyper-competitive world is to ensure your branding is spectacular from the very beginning. Imagine how soul-crushing it would be if your channel art wasn't optimized, and your reach was reduced to a mere trickling of individuals visiting your channel. The main question to ask yourself is... *what incentive are you giving people to come back?* You don't want to tarnish your reputation early because you will discourage your viewers from returning to your channel and watching future videos. In summary, it's always a good idea to put your best food forward right from the start.

## 3. Optimize Videos for YouTube Search

The only reliable way for anyone to grow a small YouTube channel organically from 0 to 1000 subscribers is by optimizing your videos for YouTube search. How do we do that, you might ask? Well, to answer that question, let's first look at how the YouTube search results function works.

There are 10 main components that YouTube uses to determine which videos are displayed on the search results page:

1. Title
2. Description   **These 3 should ideally ALL match!**
3. Tags
4. Subtitles
5. Keyword Groupings
6. Channel Relevancy
7. Channel Authority
8. Video Authority
9. Exclusivity
10. Urgency

The <u>title, description, and tags</u> will be some of the first items you focus on during the video upload process, which we will cover in much greater detail in Module 4. And ideally, you will want all three of these components to match. And what I mean by that is that the exact strings of words you use in your video titles should match the words in your description and tags as well. For example, if your video title is "5 Best Stores To Shop Using EBT", you'll want your description to mention the words "shop using EBT". Similarly, you'll also want to include the words "shop using EBT" as an exact tag while posting your video. As you can see, I took a string of words directly from my video title and word-for-word copied and pasted them directly into my video description and tags, so they all matched each other.

The next component I want to explain are video subtitles. As a courtesy to your viewers, it's always wise to remember to *enable subtitles for EVERY video you post on your channel.* Not only will this help viewers with disabilities, but it's also a great way to improve your channel's overall reach by connecting you with international audiences. YouTube allows you to select subtitles for your video in any world language. Later in Module 3, we'll cover some unique and powerful strategies you can apply using subtitles.

YouTube will also take keyword proximity and keyword grouping matches into consideration. Think of it this way… When you're talking about "ingredients to bake a cake", you might use the words "flour", "sugar", and "icing". That's a keyword grouping. These are the expected keywords the average person would likely enter into the search bar, provided they were interested in the ingredients needed to bake a cake. But if your videos are missing these keywords, chances are your video will rarely be seen because there are plenty of other channels that *DO* use them. If you think a little deeper about it, it all makes sense. YouTube wants to recommend videos they can positively affirm will be both relevant and interesting to a potential viewer. In saying that, why would YouTube take any chances on a video that doesn't contain all the most common keywords for a relevant video category? The short answer is… they wouldn't.

So how does YouTube figure out which keywords form a keyword grouping? Great question. By comparing thousands of videos for a particular topic and searching for similarities. But how do you ensure your video passes the keyword grouping test? Another great question! Oh wait, I forgot I'm the one writing this… I guess I'm an expert at asking myself great questions. You'll want to watch some of the best-ranking videos created by other similar YouTubers in your chosen niche. Recall what I said earlier about finding similar YouTubers to yourself with at least 500k – 1M+ subscribers? Again, this will ensure you're making content people actively want to watch. And won't immediately find unrelatable to them. When you're studying other channels and YouTubers in your niche, pay attention to and identify popular keywords they use, so you can apply the same ones to your videos. This includes any keywords you use for your video scripts, titles, descriptions, tags, etc. Obviously, you don't want to mimic the exact same titles other YouTubers use, but identify common keywords and form your own unique titles around them. Identify what gaps exist and fill them.

Next up, we have <u>Channel Relevancy</u>. Besides the video itself, YouTube will also want to consider the overall theme of your YouTube channel. Do you regularly create videos around a specific topic or theme? *The more videos you make about a certain topic or theme, the higher your channel's relevancy grows.* This is because YouTube wants to lower the risk of recommending videos to people who don't know what they're talking about.

As a companion to Channel Relevancy, we have <u>Channel Authority</u>. Your Channel Authority is essentially your social proof on YouTube. If your video has a good track record in terms of engagement, then YouTube is more likely to recommend your videos to new viewers because they see you as a lower risk. But how do you prove that to YouTube? You can do that by consistently creating videos with a high-authority score, meaning YouTube can see in the comments section that viewers trust and respect what you have to say. This is also why it's essential that you *speak with a clear tone and with conviction.*

Here's a hard pill to swallow, but it is probably one of the most significant pieces of advice in this entire book. No one will believe, let alone listen to what you have to say, unless you have supreme confidence in what you are saying. The world doesn't have time for non-committal behavior. To come out on top, you must overcome any personal uncertainty or anxiety about being in front of a camera. And be real with yourself. If you don't think you can do it or you're unsure of yourself, you will find it very challenging to make any progress. Instead, you need to *think like a shark*. When sharks want something, they chase it, kill it, and eat it. And do it again and again and again. When a fish wants something, it swims around and gets pummeled around by the current, and eventually gets eaten by something higher up in the food chain. In summary... be a shark, not a fish.

Next up on our list is <u>Video Authority</u>. When you're first starting, your videos will likely appear to lack any authority. In other words, YouTube won't know at first glance if your video is any good or bad. How would it know? YouTube has no historical data on you, so it can't yet figure out if you are worth being promoted to other viewers. Drop your ego and focus on proving yourself. As users watch your videos, the higher your videos will score, which we will discuss in further detail later in Module 3.

This leads us to our next topic of discussion: <u>Exclusivity</u>. The best way to accomplish exclusivity is by having either no, or as little competition as possible. If your video is so unique that no one has made anything about that topic before, YouTube may very well recommend it. In the best-case scenario, this could lead to you gaining hundreds of thousands, if not millions of views. As I mentioned earlier in this book, that's precisely why I recommend using TubeBuddy. This tool allows you to identify not only the most common keywords users are searching for, but also which ones are competitive. TubeBuddy predicts how challenging it would be for you to rank higher in the search results, based on how many other channels are using the same specific keyword or phrase. So, as more people watch your videos, YouTube will concurrently collect more data points for the algorithm to learn exactly *who* enjoys watching your videos. This provides YouTube with the tools it needs to recommend your videos to viewers that are actively searching for your type of content.

The last, and final component that I firmly believe is essential to enhancing your videos… is Urgency.

Many would agree the sign of a productive person is someone who works with a sense of urgency. Working with a sense of urgency has multiple positive benefits, some of which may contribute to propelling you even faster into success. More importantly, it allows you to defeat your opponents. In the competitive universe of YouTube, *the early bird ALWAYS gets the worm.* And what I mean by that is when you're posting videos on Topic X, you will want to focus on being the very *FIRST* to post about it. Because again… you are generating video authority! So, the next time someone searches for Topic X, your video will appear at the top of the search index. As a bonus, this also forces your competitors to work twice as hard to try and beat you. See how that works?

Now that we've covered the 10 main components YouTube uses to determine which videos are displayed on the search results page, we will discuss some science behind the YouTube algorithm. Let's say you search for: "How to make money on YouTube." What does YouTube do next? Well, a lot of this information is proprietary. From what I've been able to deduce, speaking solely from experience, YouTube will take your search phrase and crunch it into their AI system to understand what the user is looking for. From there, YouTube will scour through its vast database of videos and pinpoint relevant ones using the keywords entered in the search bar.

One of YouTube's primary goals is to ensure that each video that gets posted is genuine. Several people figured out a way to game the system. In the early days of YouTube, some folks recognized that they could use extremely clickbaity titles, even if they little or sometimes nothing to do with the video at all. This allowed early Creators to trick people into clicking on their videos, raking in thousands if not millions of views, as a result.

Imagine clicking on a video titled: "How to eat healthy so you can live 10 years longer" and when you proceeded to watch the video, you discovered it was something entirely different. To prevent this from continuing, YouTube curated its algorithm.

So how does the YouTube algorithm typically handle a user's search? And how do we ensure our channel is optimized for our niche so a viewer can easily search for the content that's most relevant to them? The way it works is that *YouTube will take a viewer's search term and try and locate it somewhere in the attributes of your video*, like your title or description. YouTube will not perform an exact match, but it will use its AI to understand its general meaning. For example, the following 4 search phrases might have identical search intent. However, if someone searched for phrase 1, a video containing phrase 3 may be displayed to them. And any combination thereof.

- Eating healthy to live longer

- Living a longer life by eating healthy

- Healthy eating habits that lead to longer life expectancy

- How to eat to live longer

As I mentioned earlier in this guide, I use TubeBuddy to identify the most optimal YouTube video titles, ideas, descriptions, and tags. I get away with using the free version, but if you want to pay for premium, it will grant you access to even better tools. However, if you're on a limited budget like me, the free version is certainly sufficient as well.

With that, ladies, and gentlemen, we wrap up the second module of this book. At this point, you should have been able to successfully set up and optimize your YouTube channel. If so, you are now ready to move on to learning how to create videos designed to reach the greatest number of people, including how to maximize video watch time.

*"Knowing is not enough, we must apply. Willing is not enough, we must do…"*

-Johann Von Goethe

# Module 3: How To Post Videos for MAXIMUM WATCH TIME!

Alright, hustlers! Assuming you were paying close enough attention in Modules 1 and 2, you should be confident that you've created a BADASS YouTube channel! Now let's analyze a couple of case studies, where I will break down three of my own YouTube channels as examples. In these examples, I will reveal some secret strategies you have likely not heard anywhere else. And especially not from the "YouTube marketing gurus." The only reason I'm aware of these strategies, and decided to share them with you, is because from the beginning I promised you complete and utter transparency. In this next section, I'm going deep into the world of YouTube and providing you with all the unique tips and tricks I learned by carefully studying

YouTube's analytics and identifying certain techniques over the years of building my own channels.

By now, I hope you've been able to extract some meaningful value out of this book. You'll want to pay extra close attention to this module, as it is crucial to your eventual success on YouTube. Even if you adhere to all the other steps from the other modules to a tee, you will still most likely fail if you don't follow this one.

Let's discuss step-by-step exactly how to post the most powerful video you can, to maximize your watch time. This should be at the very TOP of your priority list if you're serious about earning money on YouTube because *watch time, views, and revenue often go hand-in-hand.*

Due to the inaccuracies over the search feature and thumbnail mishandling, YouTube responded by tweaking its algorithm to weigh more significantly on the watch time of your video. So, what is watch time? Well, it's exactly how it sounds. The time that a viewer watches your video. So obviously, the longer your watch time, the longer the average viewer spends watching your video. And that allows advertising companies to insert even more ads and achieve even greater ad watch time on your videos. That's also a valuable lesson in business. When you can provide value to the big institutions and make them richer, you'll find it will almost always pay off for you too! The equation for going viral is *trying to get as close to 100% watch time as possible and creating the most eye-catching thumbnails in your video category.* This is precisely the strategy Mr. Beast uses to make his videos go viral. If you want to boil down the entire process of succeeding on YouTube to two main components: it's your *watch time* and your *thumbnail.* Because think about it… when you open YouTube and watch a video, what has your brain registered between the time you initially opened YouTube and the time you closed it again? Well, when you first searched for a video, your brain registered seeing a thumbnail that caught your eye in the genre you were interested in watching. And when you click on a video and watch it, your brain registers the content provided in the video. And that, my friends, is the product that YouTube provides the consumer. In return for this product, YouTube generates ad revenue on these videos. So, when you think about it in logical terms, it's in your best interest to ensure your videos continue to be promoted by YouTube by accommodating as much ad space as humanly possible. At the same time, you also need to make sure you are maintaining the viewer's attention for as long as possible. Think about it like a line on a graph, where you have watch time on the x-axis and viewer attention on the y-axis. The longer your watch time, the higher your viewer retention will be. And ultimately, the more ads YouTube decides to place on your videos, the more money you will earn. Unfortunately, if your viewer retention is low, your watch time will also be lower. So, you *NEED* to focus on keeping both as high as possible if you want to be successful at this.

**SECRET STRATEGY #1**: The first secret strategy I want to share with you is something not widely advertised in mainstream media. And as I mentioned back in *Scenario 4 of Module 1*, many of us have busy lives and don't have the time or energy to constantly come up with new content for videos. As a solution to this, I promised you a channel content idea for you to freely use at your discretion. And here it is… To put it simply, *one powerful category of YouTube you can safely and consistently do… is news reporting*. And that's what I did to achieve my own YouTube success. On one of my channels, I focused on providing up-to-date news and information specifically for retirees on Social Security, SSI, and disability benefits. Why Social Security of all things? Well, because 66 million Americans currently receive Social Security benefits each month. And many of them find this information highly relevant to their lives. As a takeaway, it's important to keep in mind how large your target audience is going to be. News reporting is great because you have almost unlimited content available at your disposal online. I would also suggest you keep them abreast of the most up-to-date news by searching for articles and stories from recent events, preferably ones released within the week. Also, look for trending news stories to improve your chances of getting your video seen by the greatest number of viewers. Due to their high search volume, YouTube will often look for channels posting videos on breaking news events and consequently promote them.

**SECRET STRATEGY #2**: This next strategy I discovered by accident, but turned out to be one of the most valuable and surprising techniques I picked up to date… And because I suck at making these smooth transitions into introducing my next strategy, I'm just going to say it... I learned *you could post the same video on multiple channels and reap the benefits of further exposure from even more audience members*. The only catch, however, is you must slightly alter the content, so it doesn't appear to be a duplicate. For example, you can essentially post a video on one channel, edit it to be slightly different, and then post it on another channel without any issues. One way I figured out how to do this was by editing my videos to show more of *myself* in the frame *during the first and last 15 seconds of the video*. I also designed alternate thumbnails for the videos I posted on my second channel. Not only did I get away with posting the videos on multiple channels for further exposure, but it also opened me up to monetizing multiple YouTube channels. Which ultimately made me *MORE $$$*! Back in 2020, I created the name "Mad Money Millennial" as a sarcastic spinoff of the name used by popular news host: Jim Cramer, aka the original "Mad Money". And from this, my third YouTube channel was born. So why not just keep opening duplicate channels forever, you might ask? Well, technically, you could. But keep in mind, you'll also need to create separate Google accounts for every single channel you create, not to mention the opportunity cost you're losing in going through the growing pains of starting yet another new YouTube channel. How much time do you possibly have to post consistently on multiple channels, not to mention coming up with new ways of slightly altering parts of the video to make it look unique. It can certainly become a lot more work than you initially envision once you get down to it.

**SECRET STRATEGY #3**: This next strategy was very, very surprising, and something I can most accurately describe as an "Ah hah!" moment. And will hopefully be for you too… What I discovered was *you could easily reach new audiences in countries outside the United States on YouTube.* And grow your reach massively at scales you wouldn't even imagine. In fact, Mr. Beast implemented this same exact strategy on one of his secondary channels called: "Mr. Beast En Español". What started as an experiment, I now saw as an opportunity to apply to my news reporting channel. Therefore, I took it upon myself to *make a copy of my primary channel* and *translate it entirely into Spanish.* Everything from the titles, and descriptions of the channel, and videos were translated word-for-word. Out the other side, I had an identical channel to my main one, consisting of the same exact content, but re-branded to reach Spanish-speaking audiences too.

As a result, my channel was no longer exclusive only to the United States, but available to neighboring countries as well, including Mexico, Puerto Rico, and the Dominican Republic.

The Pyramid of YouTube Success:

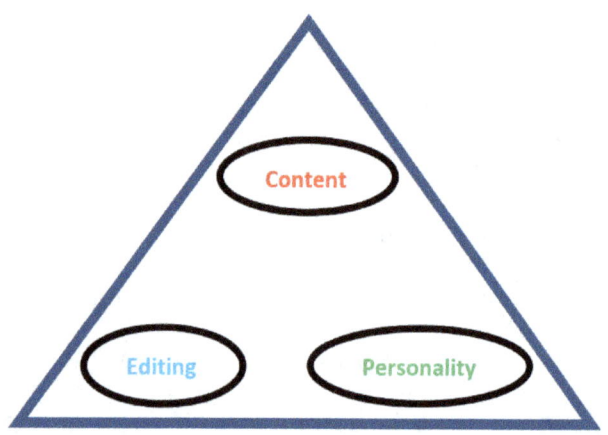

Do you remember that saying from college? "You can study, sleep, or socialize. Choose two." Well, with YouTube, the same idea applies. To make the best YouTube video, you will need to be strong in at least 2 of the 3 possible areas:

1. Producing Valuable Content

2. Professional Editing

3. Having An Outstanding Personality

Without at least 2 of the 3, I'm sorry to say you will likely lack the ability to gain any significant traction.

For this next set of techniques, we will again use my 3 channels as case studies to illustrate exactly how they work. But instead of calling them secret strategies, we will call them *key strategies*. Because for the most part, these strategies are quite common and not very secret. But they sure as heck are *KEY*!

**KEY STRATEGY #1:** The first key strategy we will discuss is using Subtitles. *Enabling subtitles is one of the simplest and most effective methods of reaching new audiences and pleasing existing ones.* It pleases existing audiences because it creates somewhat of a podcast feel, which I'm sure we can agree is one of the most popular ways people consume content in modern times. For audience members living in the USA, *the most effective and logical method for maximizing views, was to enable BOTH English and Spanish (Mexico) subtitles*, simply because the majority of people living in the United States speak those two languages. Make sense?

**KEY STRATEGY #2:** This next key strategy I'm sure you've heard on the internet at least a few times before. And that is <u>CONSISTENCY</u>. And no, I don't mean once a week. Or twice a week, or even 3 times a week. But if you truly want to make it on YouTube and are ready to make your channel pick up some serious growth, *you will have to commit to posting daily*. Yep, you heard me right. You're going to need to post one video, ideally at the same time, every single day. Don't worry about stretching it to two. But every single day, without missing a single day, you will need to post a video. Now, if you think you're going to post less than one video a day, or at different times, you will have a horrible time picking up any decent traction. The reason for this is because *YouTube favors Creators that treat their video posting schedule like it's their job...* because it is! YouTube favors hard work and dedication, just as any other job employer would. Personally, it only took me posting videos for one single week before my first video blew up on one of my channels. And it didn't even take the whole week to get there. By my sixth video, I got to experience my first-ever taste of going somewhat viral. Before this, I had only been receiving around 3-5 views per video, mostly from watching myself. But by video 6, the YouTube algorithm looked favorably on my video and decided to promote it. By the time the traffic started dying down, I had the pleasure of achieving my first 1000 views *on a single video*. And the best part of it was I hadn't watched it 1000 times myself! It suddenly dawned on me. I finally and legitimately got a video promoted by

YouTube. When a video gets promoted by YouTube, your video gets pushed by the fabled YouTube recommendations. The more this happens, the greater the chances for someone genuinely interested in your niche to stumble across your videos. This is the reason why *you need to make sure you post consistently!* That is the only way you will get the kind of traffic you need to get your channel to grow fast. One of the hardest parts of running a YouTube channel is ensuring your viewers are constantly entertained, because getting them hooked to your channel is just the first piece of the puzzle. Ideally, you want your viewers to 1) Watch your videos all the way through and 2) Keep coming back to watch every new one. Keep in mind this will not be possible to achieve every single time you post new content. But the closer you can get to achieving these two things, the faster your channel will grow. And the more momentum you can generate.

**KEY STRATEGY #3:** The third key strategy I want to share with you is *how to choose a terrific* _Thumbnail_. As we mentioned earlier in this book, you can almost entirely boil your success on YouTube down to two simple things: your watch time and thumbnail. As we discussed in Module 2 regarding the various options associated with your channel banner, the same applies to your thumbnail. So, depending on your unique budget, it's up to you to decide which option to go with.

1. Make your thumbnail using a computer program like Microsoft Paint or Word. While this is the least recommended option, this option is free. Not only that, but there is plenty of stock footage online and basic customization features these programs come with, which should be sufficient for you to design a decent-looking thumbnail. Now,

when I say, "decent," this is not how you will get the best possible "bang for your buck". The reason is that, even if it's free, the time cost associated with you trying to create your thumbnail can often make the process tedious and hardly worth it. Remember, *don't give up too much of your time opportunity cost when developing content.* We want to keep things simple because, with YouTube, the smoother you can make things for yourself, the less stress you will put on yourself and ultimately, the more you will enjoy the experience. And that's what it's all about! :D

2. The next option you have is to purchase some decent thumbnail design software. This is what I do for my own YouTube thumbnails.

Picmaker is an excellent program for starters. Their monthly memberships are affordable too. The one I use only costs me about $10 a month. You can use the software to add an eye-catching background. Add some shapes, text, enhancements… Get creative with it! If you have the time to learn, plenty of tutorials (on YouTube, ironically) can teach you how to design a professional thumbnail from scratch!

3. If you're the lazy type or have some spare money to throw around, you could opt for the most expensive option. And that's to hire a thumbnail artist on a freelancer site like Fiverr or Upwork. One of the most beneficial things about this

option is you can guarantee yourself the highest possible quality. Instead of ending up with something amateurish or pixelated, a professional artist will provide you with a crisp, high-resolution image. Be clear with whoever you hire that the sizing of the thumbnail should be precisely 1280 X 720 pixels to ensure it fits nicely in the frame.

With your chosen thumbnail creation process in mind, let me get into another trick I discovered while growing my second YouTube channel. *Use the same thumbnails in alike videos!* And when I say the same, I mean the *exact same thumbnail.* To be straight with you, I got bored of coming up with brand new thumbnails every single time I had to post a new video. And even more tired of coming up with unique text to add to these thumbnails. To solve this issue, I experimented with posting different thumbnails for news videos on the same topic... And the funniest part about it was it worked! Here's what I did... Remember how I said I made videos that addressed low-income earners that struggled with food insecurity? Well, as a way of grabbing my target audience's attention, I strategically added the following giant bold letters to all my thumbnails: "SNAP, EBT, & P-EBT RECIPIENTS...LISTEN UP". What I'm trying to do here is directly address my target audience. Therefore, *I would purposely re-use the same exact thumbnails whenever I posted a new video*, but only if it related to the same general topic. For my Social Security videos for example, I would make it a point to re-use the same exact Social Security-themed thumbnail, every time I posted a video on that topic. As a result, I was able to reduce the overall time I took to crank out a video, which increased my overall efficiency and lowered my chances of fatigue.

**KEY STRATEGY #4:** For our fourth key strategy, I want to focus on scriptwriting. How do you formulate scripts, so your videos garner decent watch time? How do you organize your thoughts into nice flowing words you can read from while you film? Well, the first step is to *create a powerful intro that draws your viewers in*, not just because they're mildly interested, but because they *NEED* to keep watching. The first 10-15 seconds of your video is *THE* most important section you need to focus on, so you must design it in a way that most of your viewers are encouraged to continue watching as far into the video as possible. And all that begins with a *HOOK!* How are you going to hook your viewers in? To put it simply, your hook should deliver a powerful message that makes the audience crave more. The other major component of your hook will be your introduction. In your introduction, you want to establish something we've mentioned several times in this book already... *Channel Authority!* Again, I will refer to one of my YouTube channels to demonstrate this strategy. The hook I personally use in the beginning of my videos is the following... "What's going on my friends! Josh Baldwin here, from Mad Money Millennial... In this video, we are going to talk about..." As you can see, I always start with a *big fat greeting.* Make your audience excited to see you! Following your greeting, I acknowledge my audience as "my friends." Because they are! *The more you can establish a good rapport with your audience members, the more they will feel connected with you.* And this connection goes a long way towards building a healthy para-social relationship between the audience and your content. That's what ensures they are invested in you as a Creator and contributes to the cult following that you can conveniently rely on when channel traffic is low. Therefore, having a channel that can positively affect your audience will likely continue to benefit you and bring you success into the future.

Following your introduction, you want to establish your credibility. After I say, "What's going on guys, Josh Baldwin here...", you'll notice I say, "...from Mad Money Millennial." What does this mean? When you initially talk to your audience, they won't know who you are. Therefore, you need to *GIVE THEM* a reason to listen to you. In my experience, *the most effective way of establishing credibility is by giving the audience the impression that you belong to a brand*. What if you don't have a brand? Create one! You are a Creator, after all. Following your hook and intro, you'll notice I say, "In this video, we are going to talk about...." Why? Because you need to tell your viewers what your video is talking about! These are good rules to live by when you write your scripts because, as we discussed, it will establish rapport and trust with your audience.

Moving onto the body of your script, this is more of an iterative and creative process that will be unique to you and your audience. As you put out more videos, you will naturally pick up a style of storytelling your audience likes. Wrapping this up, let's talk about the final piece to the puzzle… your outro. The outro will follow somewhat of a similar format to your intro. Once again, I would suggest you introduce yourself and your brand. As your audience finishes watching your video, you want them to remember who you are. So, remind them! The next part of your outro, and you've likely heard this before… is to directly ask your audience to click the "Like" and "Subscribe" buttons. I highly recommend you ask your audience to do this *BOTH at the beginning and end of your videos.* In my personal experience, I like to sneak it in about 30 seconds into the video, right after my intro. And about 30 seconds before the end of the video, right before my outro. You'll notice your viewer retention will largely drop off as you announce your outro. Therefore, it's most optimal to promote yourself right before that. When it comes to scriptwriting, one very helpful thing to also remember is that *a full page of single-spaced, size 11 font will yield approximately 4 – 5 minutes of video length*. Therefore, to reach the 8 – 10-minute mark, you will want to fill about two full pages worth of content. Remember that as you form your scripts. But what is the ideal video length?

**KEY STRATEGY #5**: By now, you've learned some of *THE* most powerful and hidden strategies for keeping your audience's eyes glued to the screen. For our fifth and final strategy, we will discuss the ideal length for a YouTube video. The length of your video often varies by topic. So how long should your video be to maximize your chances of success?

The short answer is - *IT DEPENDS!*

Some Creators have found success in longer-form content, while others in shorter-form. Quoting Statista's report, the average YouTube video length is approximately 11.7 minutes. According to the Social Media Examiner, "In general, videos between 7-15 minutes perform better." At the same time, you need to get straight to the point without forcing viewers to sit unnecessarily through a fluffy and longer video. For example, a how-to video might need to be five minutes long, while a testimonial video could be just thirty seconds long. Generally, and based on the most current rules (in 2023), I would *shoot for at least 8 minutes without getting too boring*. That last part, "without getting too boring," is important! Remember, the goal is to make your video's watch time as long as possible. *BUT* don't try and force it if it doesn't have enough "meat" for an 8-minute video. You never want to make a video longer for the sake of making it longer because you'll risk repeating yourself and annoying your audience with the redundancies. Don't worry if your video is 9 or 12 minutes long instead of exactly 8; it won't make much difference. YouTube is primarily concerned with whether your content is *watchable.*

**Monetized YouTubers Only\*\*:** Let's stop for a minute to discuss ad placements related to video length. However, to capitalize on this information, you will need to already be a member of the YouTube partner program. For maximum revenue, *you want to make your video last at least 8 minutes long because it gives you the additional option of adding mid-roll ads in your videos.* You can place as many mid-roll ads in your video as you want. However, you will also need to identify a perfect balance for optimal viewer experience. Because if you place too many ad breaks, you risk a drop-off in retention rates. In fact, I have seen a strong correlation between drop-off points and ad breaks in my audience retention graphs. Therefore, you need to determine the most appropriate points to place your ads in to avoid these drop-offs. YouTube gives you the option of adding pre-roll, mid-roll, and post-roll ads. The post-roll ads are switched off by default, but ideally, you want to use all three to maximize your video revenue. No matter the video length, if you put in the time and effort to optimize your content, you will be setting up your videos for maximum exposure! Something I have seen other Creators do is purposefully let the audience know when an ad break was coming up. The bottom line is, *you need to place your ads at appropriate times to retain the most revenue and the most of your audience's attention.*

As a final note on this chapter, if it feels like you lack any decent creativity for making videos in your chosen genre, don't beat yourself about it. Keep at it, and your skills will grow. Being creative and original is an art form that takes time and practice, just like anything else in life. As a side note, remember that *the ability to take constructive criticism and feedback in the comments section is extremely important for sustainable growth of your channel.*

*"The more powerful and original a mind, the more it will incline towards the religion of solitude..."*

-Aldous Huxley

# Module 4: How to Post Videos to Maximize the Visibility of Your BRAND!

Alright, my friends, for our fourth and final module, we will be learning how to post videos to maximize the visibility of your YouTube channel and *YOUR BRAND*. That's *YOU!* By now, you should be well-versed on topics such as choosing a powerful niche that suits you, creating and optimizing your first-ever YouTube channel, and how to post videos for maximum watch time. Assuming you've read through and understood Modules 1 – 3, you are now ready to learn the skills and strategies of video promotion and advertising, which will help you grow your channel tremendously and reduce any risk of plateau or delay in growth.

It's no secret that the more exposure you get, the more views you acquire and, ultimately, the more money you earn. The highest earners know their brand is their most valuable and powerful asset. From the very beginning of your YouTube journey, you *NEED* to be aggressively pushing your brand at every chance you get. Remember what we covered back in Module 3. You need to treat your YouTube channel *like a real business* if you want to develop any significant traction. Because it will be treated as such by the YouTube algorithm. For example, if you aren't posting consistently at the same times each day, you will likely find it difficult to sustain any long-term growth. Besides posting consistently, what other tactics can you use to your advantage so you can get monetized the soonest? Well, you have a couple of options, which are equivalent in terms of their effectiveness at helping you grow to reach 1000 subscribers. You can implement one of these tactics or a few. But if your goal is to minimize the time to reach monetization, I would recommend applying all of them. Now buckle up, take out a pen and paper, and jot these notes down... As we mentioned back in Module 2, *a great YouTube channel starts with great SEO*. And great SEO starts with understanding what users are looking for. People don't just look for videos on YouTube; they use Google too. Google now prioritizes video over other content in their algorithm for many searches. There's no set rule for which keywords will help your YouTube video rank well, but reverse engineering can go a long way. One trick I highly recommend is typing the first word of the subject you want to talk about into the search bar of either Google or YouTube and seeing what comes up. The words recommended afterward will typically give you a decent hint or idea as to what kind of titles are good candidates. And that brings us to our second strategy… Using concise but descriptive video titles. What's the *VERY FIRST THING* your viewers see when they click on your channel or come across your video? Your *TITLE!* Your title will plant an idea in your viewer's head as to what the subject matter of your video is. The following are 3 tips for forming strong video titles:

**1) Keep it short and sweet.**

Popular YouTube videos tend to have shorter titles. Stick to 60 characters or less because some of your titles may get cut off when displayed on a mobile phone, where the screen size is a lot smaller than a laptop or a TV. *Include your keyword(s) in the first half of the title* so the viewer (and YouTube) can understand what your video is about. Also, keep in mind *most online readers tend to scan the beginning of the sentence and skip the rest.* Remember that making something engaging does NOT mean you should make it appear clickbaity. The best headlines offer an obvious benefit or invoke an emotional or dramatic reaction in your viewer's mind. While clickbait can certainly be tempting, it can also damage your channel's reputation in the long term. Being genuine and acting "in good faith" goes a long way in establishing and building trust with your audience.

## 2) Add a category to the beginning of the title, followed by a colon and the subject of the video.

This is more of a recommended strategy rather than a hard rule. And although it works, it's not always necessary for forming good video titles. The way this strategy works is to *keep the beginning of your title the exact same every single time you post a video, followed by a colon and the specific subject of your video.* And what this does is effectively categorize your videos so the almighty YouTube algorithm can learn what your videos are talking about. At the same time, you'll want to make sure your title category is general enough. Don't be too specific.

For example, for my videos on Social Security benefits, the beginning of my titles would say "SOCIAL SECURITY UPDATE:". Notice the colon placed right after the category of the video. As I explained earlier, this helps YouTube predict what kind of content you put out and what kind of audience to recommend your videos to.

**3) Add a sense of urgency to it.**

When trying to figure out the perfect video title, you'll want to invoke a sense of urgency in the viewer. What I mean by that is you want to give the viewer a *REAL* reason to click on your video, because this improves what's known as your CTR, or "click-through rate." Click-through rate is the percentage of people who clicked on your video after seeing your thumbnail. Here's an example: If 10,000 people see your video somewhere on YouTube, but only 200 people click on it, that's a 2% click-through rate. That means 2% of people who scrolled by your video were interested enough to click on it. In my experience, you want your CTR to be at least 15% if you want to expand your reach beyond your current subscribers. However, ideally, you want your CTR to be at least 20% if you want to be promoted further by YouTube recommendations. YouTube recommendations are important because that is where you will typically earn the bulk of your overall channel views. Going back to forming strong video titles, *one of the most effective emotions to invoke in the viewer when they first read your title… is fear.* If you add something fear-inducing in your video title, you increase the chances the viewer will want to see your video because they will be intrigued by the unanswered questions now looming in their mind after reading your title. Their craving to learn more in combination with their interest in the subject makes a well-titled video very difficult to resist.

Besides alluring video titles, there are several other concepts you will need to consider. Thumbnails, editing, tags.... There's a laundry list of things I can get into on how to improve your traffic by a larger percentage each time you post a new video. But I figure it would be a lot more helpful if we got right into some of the most crucial *KEY* strategies you'll need to learn if you want to attract large amounts of traffic to your channel.

**KEY STRATEGY #1:** Streamlining your video uploads is an essential skill for every Creator to learn if they want to be successful on YouTube. In fact, the process of pushing outside viewers to your channel begins the very moment you hit the "Upload" button. Now, there are a couple of steps to remember when it comes to uploading a YouTube video. And the better you follow these steps, the greater you improve your video's chances of getting seen. This is because *YouTube* *is designed so that every single tag you use and every selection you make during the video upload process will directly affect how many people see your videos.*

If you're ready to upload your YouTube video, please go to <u>YouTube.com</u> so you can follow along!

1. The first step to uploading a video on YouTube is by clicking the video camera icon in the top right corner and clicking "Upload".

2. After that, tap the "SELECT FILES" button and select the video you want to upload from your computer. This will open "YouTube Studio", where you will proceed with the rest of the upload process.

3. At our first screen where it says "Title", enter your carefully crafted video title. If you still need help forming good titles, refer a little earlier in this module, where

we covered 3 main tips for forming strong video titles.

4. The next step is to fill out the <u>video description</u>. How do we do that exactly? We covered how to create effective titles, but how do we do the same with the video description?

   a. One way is by utilizing "Hashtags" at the top of the description field. Hashtags assign your video to a certain category and lump you in with other videos that are using similar ones. Like the video title strategy that we just covered, in which you add a category followed by a colon, adding hashtags produces a similar effect in helping YouTube determine exactly where to push your videos.

5. The next item on our list is the <u>YouTube Thumbnail</u>. To upload your thumbnail, click the "Upload thumbnail" button and locate your wonderful artwork on your computer. If you still need help designing a stunning thumbnail, please refer to *Key Strategy #3, located in Module 3.*

   a. Remember, with YouTube, it's not always a bad idea to keep your thumbnails consistent. Don't be afraid to recycle them in future videos; you could even use the same thumbnail repeatedly (just don't forget to update any outdated language). Not only does this free up time for you, but recall it also allows the YouTube algorithm to learn what your videos are about!

   b. You will also want to make sure your thumbnails match the general theme of your video. So, if you're posting cooking videos, you ideally want to use a cooking-themed thumbnail. You get the idea...

c. Keep the perfect amount of vagueness in your thumbnail. Going back to the cooking example, the kind of text and artwork you use should be tailored toward a larger, broader audience rather than a smaller, narrower one. You'll want to use words like: "5 Great Stove Top Cooking Tips" rather than "Why Butter Is Better To Use Rather Than Oil On Non-Stick Pans". Include an expressive picture of yourself in the kitchen holding a fry pan rather than one that appears wordy or clunky. Get your point across with as little jargon as possible.

6. Following your thumbnail upload, we need to make our <u>playlist selections</u>. Playlists are basically collections, or groupings of videos of a similar topic. YouTube allows you to create your own playlists and name them whatever you like. Going back to the cooking example again, good examples of relevant playlist collections might be things like: "Spice Tips", "Baking Essentials", "Favorite Desserts", and so on...

    a. Like hashtags, *playlist selections are an excellent way of categorizing your videos to help boost your reach even further.*

    b. You can customize your channel homepage's layout to include all your favorite playlists. Go to your channel and click the "Customize Channel" button. From there, you can add some of your favorite playlists and rearrange them however you wish.

c. One strategy I would highly recommend for maximizing the flow of traffic to your channel is by *creating a playlist of your MOST POPULAR videos and pinning it at the tippy top of your channel page*! That way, you again exercise a principle we covered back in Module 2… *Channel Authority*. You want your audience to trust what you have to say when they land on your page. And to view you as a legitimate and trustworthy source. In fact, you'll notice other widely popular YouTubers, like Graham Stephan, also apply this strategy. Big hint in my opinion!

7. Next on our list in the Upload Process is the <u>Audience</u> section. If you're making videos specifically for children, you'll want to click the "Yes" option here. Otherwise, you will usually want to check the "No" option by default. That's all you need to know about this section. If you don't want to make this selection every time you upload a video, you can skip this part by going into your settings and setting the default option there.

8. For this next section, you will obviously want to check the "Yes" option if you're promoting any product or service; or doing any sort of sponsorship or brand deal. Otherwise, feel free to skip this part.

9. <u>Automatic chapters and places</u> are two options you'll notice will automatically be checked. And you'll want to keep them that way. You also have the option of creating

your own custom chapters, which viewers love because it allows them to skip straight to the juicy parts of your video. So how do you create your own custom chapters? This is especially useful for long-form content because it helps you avoid boring your audience with the parts of your video that are irrelevant to them. When I'm watching a longer form video, I personally appreciate when a Creator takes the time to place chapters so I can quickly locate the content I'm looking for.

a. So where do we add our custom chapters? The location where you add your chapters is inside the Video Description box.

b. What is the basic format for adding Chapters? First, you'll want to break each part of your video down into separate sections, each with their own individually assigned time stamps. These time stamps will show to the precise second when each section begins in the video. To summarize, *the basic format for creating custom chapters is a time stamp, followed by a dash, and ending with the assigned chapter name.* Begin a new line, add the time stamp at which the next section starts, followed by a dash, and ending with the name of that assigned chapter.

**Chapters:**

0:00 – Introduction

2:35 – Segment 1

5:50 – Segment 2

10:23 – Segment 3

Once you finish doing this, you'll notice you now have the option of skipping directly to each of the sections you assigned in your custom chapter list. Your video will also be able to stand out a lot easier on the YouTube search pages because your chapters will now be displayed in the previews of those videos. Remember, even though some of these details may seem minor, YouTube's algorithm is quite advanced and will take notice of every detail you add, or don't add, to your videos.

10. Next up, we will cover <u>Tags</u>. Contrary to a lot of other opinions on the internet, I take tags quite seriously. The concept that tags are an old-school, outdated feature, used back when YouTube relied more heavily on keywords is an uninformed way of looking at things. I use tags, again, to allow YouTube to learn how to categorize my videos. *YouTube will display videos to viewers containing similar, if not the same tags, to more*

*accurately recommend videos that they believe those viewers will enjoy.*

a.  If you're posting videos of a similar category to a previous one, you'll want to recycle the same exact tags each time. This helps the YouTube algorithm to not have to try and re-learn how to categorize your videos every single time you post a new one. Instead, your next video will automatically be linked to the previous one in which you applied those same tags. This ultimately leads to your video getting recommended to even more viewers who are searching for content related to those tags. See how that works?

b.  So, what's the easiest way to find the tags from the last video you posted so you can copy them over to the new one? Great question... The simplest way of grabbing recent tags is by opening YouTube on a separate tab from the one you're currently posting your video on. From there, navigate to your channel and click "Manage Videos." Click the Edit button on the video you want to grab your Tags from. Scroll down until you see the tags section and click the "Copy" symbol to copy them to your Clipboard. And WALLA! Now you can go back to the tab where you were posting your video and paste them right in.

11. The next few sections: <u>Recording Date and Location, License and Distribution, and Shorts sampling,</u> aren't relevant to this

book. For these, I would suggest simply leaving the default option as-is.

12. Next up, we will cover the <u>Category</u> section. Adding a video to a Category is essential, as it allows YouTube to place your video appropriately in front of the right people.

   a. From the drop-down menu, click the category that aligns *MOST* with the content in your video.

13. Under <u>Comments and Rating</u>, you can determine what kind of comments you will allow on your YouTube videos. Unless you feel compelled to be more, or less stringent, with the kind of comments that appear underneath your videos, I would opt to leave the default option enabled on this one as well.

And that, my friends, covers the first set of steps in the video upload process. Once ready, click the

"Next" button to proceed to the <u>Video Elements section</u>.

14. In 2023, YouTube added a new feature where you can add <u>music tracks</u> to your videos directly from the Creator music library. That way, you can safely add music to your video without the risk of having your video potentially muted or marked ineligible for monetization. Personally, I leave this feature alone because I like to add my own music tracks. Whatever you choose to do, just *make sure you're following copyright guidelines.* You never want to miss out on monetizing a video, nor risk a strike against your channel, simply because you misused a track or audio file.

15. Next up, we have the option to add <u>Subtitles</u>. Back in Module 2, we briefly introduced subtitles as one of the 10 main components YouTube uses to determine

which videos get displayed in the search results.

    a. One unique and powerful strategy I personally discovered, which made a profound impact on my reach was *enabling both English and Spanish (Mexico) subtitles.* Why exactly? Statistically, Spanish is the most common language spoken in the United States besides English, with around 41 million speakers. Enabling subtitles in Spanish allows a whole new populace of viewers the opportunity to watch and understand your video. And if they enjoy it, who knows? Maybe an audience member with a vast social network ends up advertising your video to a whole new audience! So, through the simple action of enabling subtitles for a second language, you effectively expanded your channel's reach to target international audiences, rather than solely domestic. Pretty powerful stuff, huh?

16. Now that we've covered subtitles, let's move on to <u>End Screens.</u> An end screen is simply defined as a content piece you promote at the end of your video. Examples of an end screen would be something like another recent video or even a secondary channel.

    a. YouTube lets you import end screens as templates from other videos to simplify the process and so you don't have to add the same ones twice. You can also click "Add" and make your own custom end-screen selections. Either way works, but I prefer the latter option so I can place them towards the end of the video. That way, your viewer gets a popup recommending them even more content to watch once they're done watching the current video.

b. I would recommend adding an end screen to your video's last 5-20 seconds, showcasing additional videos, playlists, links, and call-to-actions.

c. Adding your own custom end screens allows you to show off your latest and greatest content to your audience. Personally, I prefer to add 3 of my most recent videos as end screens. *This is also a fantastic way of recovering previously "dead" videos and getting the views to start rolling in again.*

17. The last portion of the video elements you'll want to pay attention to are <u>Cards</u>. Cards allow you to embed even more content into your video such as: a playlist, a second channel, or even a link to an external website.

    a. YouTube also allows you to decide where you want to place your cards. As a best practice, don't place your cards too early in your video... otherwise, you risk viewers clicking off your video prematurely and hurting your watch time. Remember... *the objective is to keep your watch time as high as possible.*

    b. Cards can point viewers to a specific link from a list of eligible websites and even display customized images, titles, and calls-to-action, similar to end screens.

c. Keep your cards towards the end of your video, preferably lined up with your outro/concluding remarks. One great strategy is to *create a call-to-action instructing your viewers to click on the cards, so they are incentivized to keep watching more content.* This will help you to accumulate more views and more watch-time. And if you're already monetized, more revenue.

18. Now that we've covered the video elements section, let's move on to the last step in the video upload process: <u>Checks</u>. When you upload a video, your video will be checked by YouTube. And there are essentially two components to the Checks process: Copyright and Ad Suitability.

a. During the copyright process, your video will be scanned for any plagiarized works. One example of copyright would be if you used a licensed music track or exact clip from someone else's YouTube channel. Previously, YouTube didn't have this Checks process, so if your video contained any copyright, it would simply be muted or marked ineligible for monetization.

b. What's changed? During the ad suitability check, YouTube will ask you if your video's content, title, description, or keywords contain any of the following content listed. You will then be shown a menu of content selections for you to choose from. Once you make these selections, YouTube will explicitly tell you whether your video qualifies for full or limited ad placement.

Click the "Next" button once complete.

Alright, my friends! By now, you've had the chance to see first-hand the entire video upload process from start to finish. Now, for the pièce de résistance... *HOW TO PUBLISH YOUR MASTERPIECE!*

On the publishing page, you will be given the option to choose the date and time you want to post your video and if you want to make it: "Public", "Un-listed", or "Private". If you pick the "Private" option, only you and certain people you choose can watch your video. If you pick the "Un-listed" option, essentially anyone with the video link can watch your video. Otherwise, your video is hidden from the rest of the world. This is a common option for beginner streamers because it allows them to see what it would be like to stream a real-life live video, with the additional comfort of being able to practice first, instead of streaming to a public audience directly. Finally, we have the "Public" option, in which anyone will be able to see your video once you post it, with no visibility restrictions. Once you're ready for the whole world to see your video, this is the option you will want to choose.

**KEY STRATEGY #2:** One of the most important elements of posting a YouTube video is determining whether you want to post your video now or schedule it to be posted later. If you schedule it to post later, let me tell you one very helpful trick I learned. In YouTube Studio, go over to your analytics, click on the "Audience" tab, and scroll down until you see a chart labeled: *"When your viewers are on YouTube"*. The darker purple regions will illustrate what times of the day there is a higher concentration of audience members on YouTube. Therefore, you can maximize the chances that a viewer will see your video. It's also a terrific way of being promoted by the YouTube algorithm to *post during these peak traffic times each day*, to maximize the chances of your subscribers seeing your video. It's also very important to keep in mind that *the first hour your video is released is extremely crucial* because YouTube uses the information it gathers during this time to determine if people are enjoying your video and whether to promote it.

**KEY STRATEGY #3**: Next to the "Public" option, you'll notice you have the option to set your videos as "Instant Premieres". *Instant Premieres are great because they allow you and your viewers to watch and experience your video together in real-time.* They're basically a fancy way of posting your video. And who doesn't like fancy things? Not only that, but if your viewers are subscribed and have post-notifications enabled, they will be notified the precise moment your video premiers. Viewers can also leave comments in the "live chat" window. This is super exciting, especially once your channel gets monetized, because Super Chat & Super Stickers are now eligible to be used during YouTube Premieres! Which means even more ways to earn money!

By now, you should be comfortable with the general process of posting your first-ever YouTube video. And gained some helpful insider knowledge on the best ways to widen your channel's exposure.

Let me quickly jumpstart your motivation by giving you an idea about how much money you can earn by following the concepts outlined in this book. As I promised, I offered you complete and utter transparency. So that's what I intend to do...

Let's once again revisit my YouTube channels as examples in demonstrating these numbers. Looking at the average monthly earnings across all my channels, I am currently earning around

$1000-$3000 per month. Let's take $1500 at the lower end as my monthly earning amount. And consider the number of days I post videos each month, which is about 16 days. My current posting rate is about *4 videos per week*, so if I divide my average monthly earning amount by 16, my earnings come out to about $93.75 per day. Divide that by the number of hours per day you spend working on YouTube. For me, that's roughly 5 hours per day, 3 hours less than the standard American 8-hour workday. And you're left with a result of *$18.75 an hour*. Not too shabby, huh? Especially considering you don't even need to leave your house and can practically sit on the couch all day and do this. Sounds much better than being paid minimum wage to stand in a drive-thru line, taking people's muffled orders till 1 in the morning. Am I right?

**KEY STRATEGY #4:** Let's discuss the incredible benefits of the Community tab. This is more of a provisional strategy and may not apply to you yet, because to unlock the Community tab, you will need to have at least 500 subscribers. So, if you don't have this many subscribers yet, feel free to skip ahead and go straight to the Conclusion & Closing Remarks...

I cannot stress enough the considerable importance of staying active on your channel's Community tab. In fact, something I made it a habit to do was *enter a Community Post EVERY single time I posted a new video.* Typically, I would write a short blurb about what the video is about, followed by a bombastic remark like: "Video premiering NOW! ENJOY!". Whatever words you choose, your goal should be to create a call-to-action for the person viewing your community post to go watch your video. YouTube isn't always the best at notifying your subscribers right when you upload a video. But when you submit a Community post, YouTube will directly notify your subscribers of the update. As a result, you can reach a much larger percentage of people in your audience. And with that, my friends, we wrap up our fourth and final module. At this point, you are presumably equipped with a skillset and knowledge base that very few people on this Earth have attained. And if you made it all the way through, I applaud you for taking the time to invest in yourself and take control over your destiny. YouTube can be a very difficult beast to handle and often takes a lot of grit to navigate. With that, I truly hope you'll be able to apply this knowledge base to carve out your own plans for achieving success on YouTube. Now it's time to put those plans into action!

*"What matters is how well you walk through the fire…"*

-Charles Bukowski

# Conclusion & Closing Remarks

The purpose of this book was to demonstrate exactly *how to create a YouTube channel and grow it from 0 to 1000 subscribers in under 30 days.* If you do it right, YouTube can be a sustainable passive income source, while giving you the freedom to handle whatever else you need to in life. Passive income is money earned no matter what you're doing... while you're out walking the dog, at home sleeping, or whatever else, your wealth continues to grow in the background. In saying that, never put all your eggs in one basket. As we mentioned earlier, you'll want to think of YouTube in a healthy way. Consider it a side hustle. *Don't let it consume your entire life.* Patiently work on and grow it, but *NEVER* let it hinder your primary source of income or other commitments. One other *VERY* important concept to keep in your deck of cards... *is consistency.* But here's something you haven't heard of yet. Say you have a video that's beginning to pick up and receive a lot more views than usual. How do you keep that kind of traction going? And capitalize on it so you can establish long-term, sustainable growth? The YouTube AI software scans every one of your videos and identifies familiar features in your videos. Over time, the software learns which videos are attracting more interest from viewers than others. And promotes them to even more viewers it believes will be interested in this sort of content. Therefore, it's in your best interest to *keep as many elements in your videos as consistent as you can...* from your audio, thumbnail, video format, effects, and so forth. You get the idea... If you follow these steps correctly, I'm confident you will be able to easily grow from 0 to 1000 subscribers in much less time than you think! Even if you don't reach

1000 subscribers in 30 days, don't lose hope, and think you can't ever pull off turning YouTube into a viable side, or even main hustle at some point. Speaking as a full-time 9-5'er, I guarantee you absolutely *ANYONE can do this*. Stick with it, and *you WILL eventually make money*. Some YouTube channels gain 1,000 subscribers in a matter of weeks, while others can take several months or even years to reach this milestone. But keep at it, and I promise it will pay off for you in the long run!! And provide you with an extra layer of financial security that will continue to benefit you into the future. Keep in mind: *the best videos are timeless*. Design your videos so people can continue to extract value from them, no matter when they watch it. In this shaky and uncertain post-COVID era, taking charge of your life and financial future is a very wise move on your part. As a final note, I truly wish you *ALL* the best of luck in achieving YouTube success. And always remember... *BE A SHARK! NOT A FISH!*

*"We are what we repeatedly do. Excellence, therefore, is not an act, but a habit..."*

-Aristotle